CHANGE YOUR LIFE TODAY WITH THE SECRET POWER OF COLOR

Martin Kutternik *and*
Colin G Smith

© Copyright 2015

Disclaimer

This eBook is for educational purposes only, and is not intended to be a substitute for professional counselling, therapy or medical treatment. Nothing in this eBook is intended to diagnose or treat any pathology or diseased condition of the mind or body. The authors will not be held responsible for any results of reading or applying the information.

Table of Contents

About the Authors

Martin Kutternik:

Martin Kutternik (b. 1966) is a qualified color therapist. He has an electrical engineering background and his passion and interest is in holistic technology and holistic products. He is an author, international teacher and director of his mail order business PANOSUN Ltd., supplying unique products for balance, evolution and health.

Visit his website here: http://www.panosun.org

Colin G Smith:

For over ten years Colin G Smith has been driven to find the very best methods for creating effective personal change. He is a NLP Master Practitioner, writer & author who has written several books including, "*The NLP ToolBox: Your Guide Book to Neuro Linguistic Programming NLP Techniques*" and, "*Creative Problem Solving Techniques To Change Your Life.*"

Visit his Amazon Author Page here:
http://www.Amazon.com/author/colingsmith

Alive With Color

So, you are interested in changing your life through the power of color? Let's look at what that might actually mean: We can all get stuck in life – when it feels like we are just going around in a circle with no way out and no hope for change or progress. But life itself is not a circle! It is a rhythmical process. We can observe these rhythms in our human bodies; the heart and breathing rhythms, the important rhythms of the cerebral spine fluid, the rhythm of female menstruation – and there are many other rhythms in the body. Each organ has its own rhythm, well known in Chinese medicine. It is the rhythms that create life.

Outside we can observe the rhythms of day and night, the rhythms of the week (less so these days as every day is now a potential shopping day and little of the weekend reserved for quietness and spiritual re-connection. Weekends used to have a significantly different feelings once the shops closed Saturday lunch time and everybody started focusing on weekend activities). And of course we have the rhythm of the year, with the seasons and the different qualities and colors that brings. Life is not cyclical – it is not repeating the same thing over and over again – it is an evolving, rhythmical spiral of evolution. When it is cyclical we feel stuck. When we feel balanced movement and progress, we feel well.

Life also offers metamorphosis – when one thing leads and changes to the next. This can be wonderfully observed when we notice how the green leaves on a rose metamorphose into rose petals – and we can often find that the first petal at the base of the rose is half leave and half petal. (Have a look when you are next in a flower shop.) The petals then metamorphose into the next part inside the rose where the same process can be observed. One builds up, maximises, and then changes to the next. We see this in human development also: e.g. how childhood transforms into youth and then that gets left behind and we become adults.

When we feel stuck we need a new impact to move us out of our stuck state. These impacts can come in many ways. Sometimes the human will is enough to shift us back into balance, but often we need outer help to regain balance. Any real 'medicine' helps the person in its parts and as a whole to regain balance. A balance between over-activity and under-activity.

While in incarnation we humans have Physical, Emotional, Mental and Spiritual levels. PEMS. All the levels of PEMS interact with all the other parts. Modern medicine assumes everything is physical, yet the psychologist makes everything mental/emotional. The truth is that each level affects all the other ones. If we have a spiritual crisis our emotional and mental state will be affected and even the physical body will slump and loose uprightness. Similarly if we are affected by a simple flu virus or have some other physical issue, our mental and emotional state will be affected and even our spirit will be weakened. If mental and emotional challenges hit us, we need to give our body extra support or it will crumble under the inner stress and trauma, which will also affect how we evolve spiritually. So in actuality it can be difficult to know what the root cause of a perceived problem is. *"Do I need a doctor or a therapist, a psychologist or some spiritual counselling to address the root of my problem?"* one might want to ask oneself.

TOP TIP: Check out MAP; The Co-Creative Medical Assistance Program. MAP is a comprehensive medical program that addresses our general health; any specific illness, disease or condition; injuries (serious or small); our mental health; our emotional health; and our overall well-being. It is a program that connects you with the medical unit of the White Brotherhood* where we are each "assigned" a team of physicians whose expertise best meets our individual needs.

The only things that are required to do this program are the book and your willingness to learn the program. As a program, it couldn't be more simple. With MAP you have high quality medical assistance any time day or night – and it's at no charge. See the booklist in the Resources section at the end of this book for more details.

The White Brotherhood isn't some supremacist/sexist organisation, but supports and assists mankind by ensuring that any work we do maintains its forward evolutionary motion.

Now let us look at how color can help you change your life and regain balance. Color can help you one step at a time. This is how all progress happens – think about it: move one foot forward, sense the new ground underneath, commit to the step, put some weight behind/on it, regain a new balance and a new position with the forward foot, and then release the foot that is left behind and move that forward in the same manner. One rhythmical step at a time. If it was cyclical you would not progress – life would be a treadmill.

We can support ourselves through to power of color by accessing it consciously. We can see color, yet we do not usually access its amazing power to help us propel into new states of being.

Basic Color Wheel Exercise

Have a look at our specially designed Color Wheel below, or you can go to a web-based image here:

http://www.effective-color.com

Let your eyes glance at it and allow your eyes to look a the color they feel most drawn too. Your eyes will select a color that helps balance your PEMS levels as a whole.

Color Wheel (go here for a more detailed Color Wheel ==> **http://www.effective-color.com**)

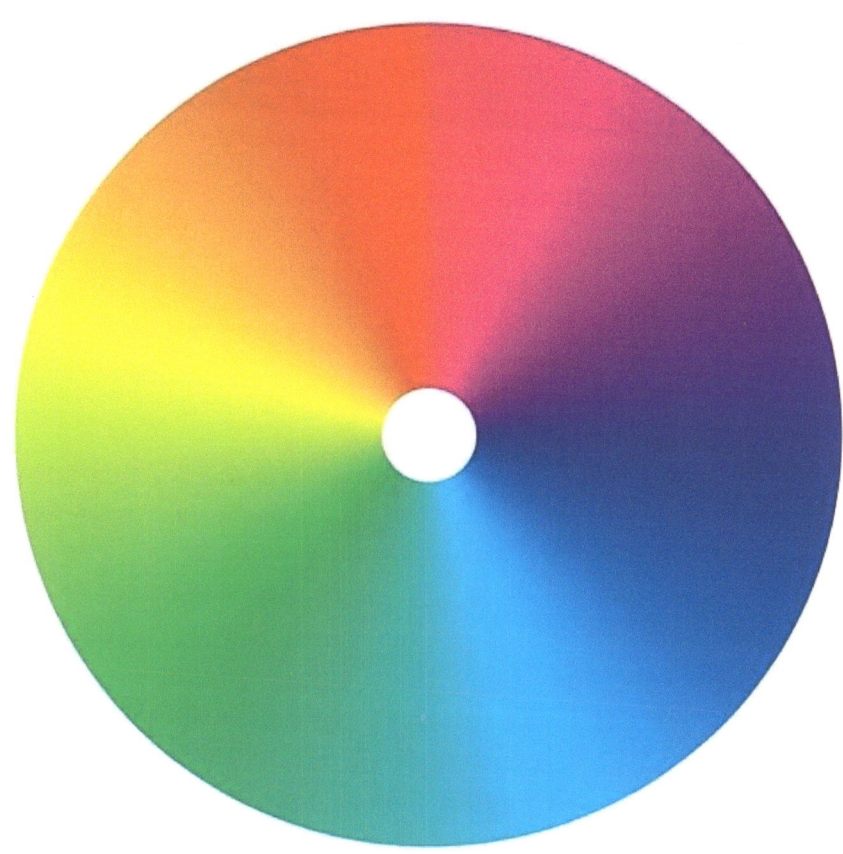

The special and absolutely real energy and quality that you receive through the eyes and the nerves leading to the brain affect glands inside the brain as part of the endocrine system (see Dr. Jacob Liberman's research and book, "Light: Medicine of the Future").

Consequentially the color you look at consciously and absorb will trigger subtle but definite changes. Not so subtle that if you looked at a selected color you will not feel different after a while, but subtle as it is a small step on the big journey of life. The more often you can do such a "balancing act", the more impulse towards change and towards balance you will help allow yourself to receive. You can do this exercise a few times in a row or 2 to 3 times a day, but we suggest you do not become a "therapy junkie", seeking to gain balance at everything you engage with. Get your vehicle into balance and ride it, and after a while, when you feel the need, rebalance it. Also when we speak of "balance" we do not mean a static situation, but a fluid and evolving one. Like you can walk in balance on a path or up a steep mountain or even walk in balance on a swaying ship. Yet if drunk, a person might fall over simply standing.

When we say balance we mean the ability to progress in a balanced way – up the rhythmical spiral of life, encountering various challenges and opportunities as they arise. Consequentially "change," to us, really means "leading to balance". Things can be changed easily – let a 2 year old toddler loose in your kitchen and it will be "changed" in no time. We aim for a change that leads to an enhancing balance that serves and supports your health, wellbeing and your ability to thrive in the life journey. A balance that supports us equally through our troublesome and challenging times, but also when we are in "comfort mode" – so we can enjoy all the phases of life better.

To really understand what color can do for you, you will need to dive into the subject. This introduction to the subject matter will give you enough background information to gain a deeper understanding and some practical experience that color is a powerful tool. So we hope this book will inform you, stretch your horizon, and serve you on your path.

Pioneers of Color

The occupation to understand the effect of colors and their use for the human being is not the latest trend. Many past civilisations realised the effect of colors and light and utilised them to aid healing. In ancient Egypt sunlight was used for medical treatments.

Hippocrates described the use of sunlight to cure various medical disorders. Although sunlight therapy had no scientific explanation at that time, the healing power of it was clear, and Roman and Arab physicians introduced light therapy for general medical use.

Today it is understood that the human body transforms light and color into electrochemical energy, which activates a chain of biochemical reactions within cells, stimulating metabolism and reinforcing the immune response of the entire human body!

Colors are also used to create certain moods at ceremonies and in rituals, to intensify and direct the experience. When we look at religious drawings and sculptures throughout the ages – we always find a deep understanding and link to the archetypes and color; i.e. the blue cloak of Mother Mary, the archetypical all loving and all accepting mother.

Some see color as the *substance of the soul*: *"feeling blue", green with envy", "rose-colored spectacles", "looking black", "seeing red",...* Others study the effect for therapeutic purposes and hope by giving color therapy a more scientific sounding name, like Chromothology, it will find wider acceptance in mainstream science.

The following pages introduce pioneering personalities in

the field of color and describe their color Philosophy. Of course there are also other people, both now and in history, who achieved breakthroughs and discovered new land in the field of color who have not been mentioned in this guide. However, a good overview shall be given through the chosen examples.

Around 1665, at the age of 23, **Isaac Newton** quarantined himself in his rooms to avoid the plague that was raging through England at the time. He discovered, when he held a prism of glass in the path of a beam of sunlight coming through a hole in the blind of his darkened room, that the white sunlight was split into red, orange, yellow, green (in the middle), cyan, blue and violet light when the light leaving the prism was "caught" by projecting it onto a surface at a certain distance, like a wall or a sheet. (Please note, that was a beam of light with *dark* boundaries!)

This led him to his theory that all colors are fractions of light and that, in reverse, all colors result in light too, as he managed to set up various experiments that would apparently show this.

Johann Wolfgang von Goethe (1749 – 1832) shows a more complete and holistic approach in his book "Theory of Color" (the original German title "Farbenlehre" was very badly translated and everybody who studied Goethe's "Theory of Color" knows that it is a study and an objective report of nature's phenomena, and not about theories at all. It is much better translated as "Color Teaching" or even "Science of Color").

Goethe always wanted to try the above mentioned Newton experiment with the prism where a room is darkened except for a small slit through which a beam of sunlight is allowed into the room. For this, Goethe borrowed a prism from the nearby University but never gotten round to setting up the experiment. As time passed, the university needed the prism back and kept sending reminders to him, urging the return. As he did not return the prism they then send a courier to his address to collect it in person.

Just as Goethe wanted to hand the prism over to the courier, he quickly glanced through the prism expecting to see beautiful rainbows wherever there was light. But he saw something quite different which he felt needed to be investigated, and therefor sent the courier away empty handed as he could not imagine giving that prism back now, just as he observed something so interesting.

During his consequential attempts to repeat Newton's light experiments he found phenomena which had not been considered before. So he diligently experimented further. Throughout his many observations and experiments, Goethe found that darkness and light are the primary essences, and that color is their creation. One could describe this as color being the *"child"* and third energy in the interplay between *"mother darkness"* and *"father light."*

If you look at the pattern of Figure 1 through a prism, you will see an image that looks like Figure 2.

Figure 1:

Figure 2:

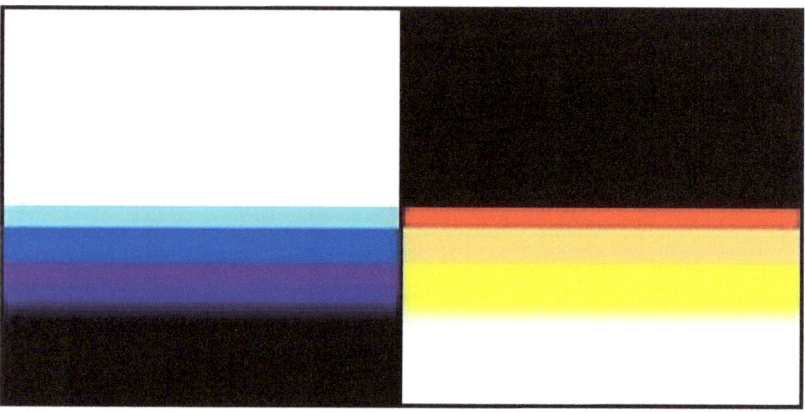

Colors appear at the points where light and darkness meet. Goethe found that the edges of light and dark overlap to certain degrees when viewed through a prism. These are the two key principles he found:

- Darkness seen through light creates turquoise (or pail blue), blue and violet (see left half of Figure 2).

- Light seen through darkness creates yellow, orange and red (see right half of Figure 2).

In this example one can imagine that the prism is "lifting"

light and darkness down, so that on the left there is light over darkness (creating the blue phenomena), and on the right darkness is over light (creating the yellow phenomena).

Green is *only* created when the two principles happen to merge, i.e. when the yellow from the one with the turquoise from the other merge. See Figure 3. In some rainbows we see white in the middle, this is the case when the two phenomena are a bit too far apart and do not meet. This white in-between, instead of green, can also bee seen in Figure 3.

Figure 3: Beam of light through prism. Notice green being created in the middle, where the two phenomena meet.

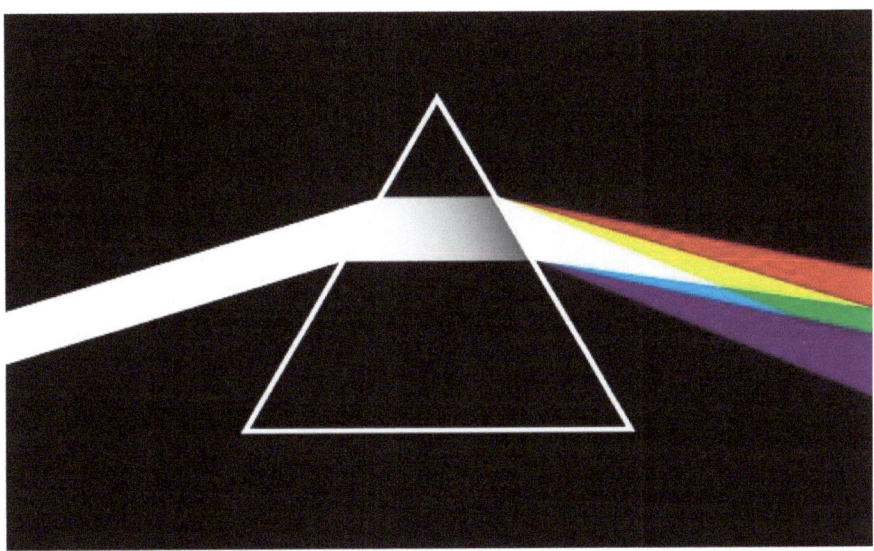

Red – Orange – Yellow – Green – Turquoise – Blue – Violet.

This is the *standard* seven color rainbow with green in the middle.

Magenta on the other hand is created where the two principles happen to meet on their other sides: I.e. red from one and violet from the other. See Figure 4.

(Please compare above image with the famous record logo of Pink Floyd's, *The Dark side of the Moon*, which shows the assumptions of Newton, that the colours emanate in the rainbow sequence right from the prism – which in reality they do not.)

Figure 4: Beam of darkness through prism. Notice magenta being created in the middle, when the two phenomena meet.

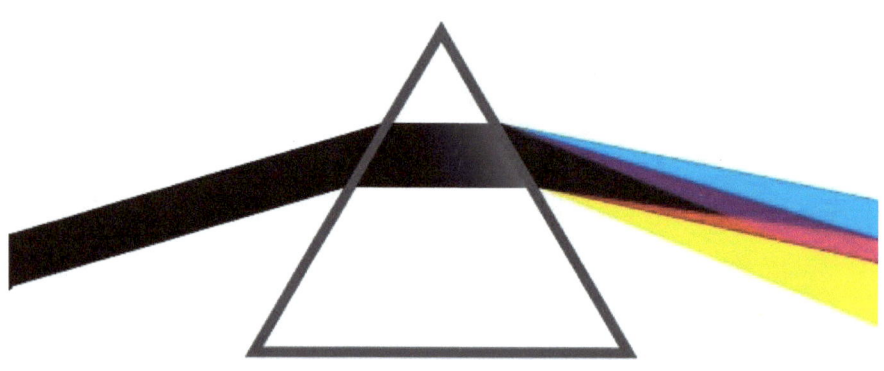

Turquoise – Blue – Violet – Magenta – Red – Orange – Yellow.

These seven colors are a different kind of rainbow. In a double rainbow it can sometimes be seen as a narrow band near one of the rainbows.

This time red (infra-red) and violet (ultra-violet) meet each other on the small dark surface in the middle and a striking magenta is produced. This is an illuminating red-pink which we often find in Cyclamen-flowers. The phenomenon of a "beam of darkness" resulting in a spectrum through the prism – a different one to what Newton observed, namely showing the colors in different order and magenta in the middle: turquoise, blue, violet, magenta, red, yellow and orange is news to most people. Notice: no green!

I understand that the described phenomena, that color arises at the edges of dark and light, and the spectrum occurs where these colored edges overlap, is something you probably did not get taught at school or university, and that therefore this concept may be bewildering and difficult to accept just now.

Magenta is a creation of the invisible "colors" ultra-violet and infra-red. In 1859 scientists experimented on the effect of both ends of the visible spectrum, red and violet meeting. The surprise was big as a reddish violet appeared from darkness – in other words from "nothing" – before the visible ends of the spectrum met each other. This "new color" in physics was named after the battle of Magenta in Italy which had just ended. These days the modern color-printing industry uses magenta as an essential basic color.

At sunrise and sunset, again when darkness and light meet, we observe a colorful intermingling of the two basic phenomena just described, especially so when clouds are added to the mix.

Observe and study a sunrise or sunset with the two principles in mind:

- Blue is created when we see darkness through light, i.e. the darkness of the cosmos seen from the earth through the light of our sun. This creates a blue image of the cosmos especially so in the morning and the evening. It is also seen during the day (during the day the blue image of the sky is also due to the fact that the earth's surrounding gasses and water vapour function like a color filter and a screen). The colors blue and violet, which follow turquoise, are created through intensifying the basic phenomena.

- Yellow is created when we see light through darkness. i.e. when we see light through a dark room, or as light creates a yellow image seen through smog or fog. The Sun we see as yellow because of the gas color filter surrounding the earth, which is in that way a bit of darkness, making the light yellow.

The colors orange and red, which follow yellow are created through intensifying the basic phenomena or seeing light trough darkness. The sun and it s light appears more orange and red if projected through clouds.

As described, green and magenta are only created when the borders of these two above phenomena meet. So we see that green and magenta are not springing directly from darkness and light, but from their "children". Green and magenta are the "grandchildren" of darkness and light.

These are basic observable phenomena of light and darkness – not theories.

Light and darkness are the primary forces behind color. All that a prism does is shift the darkness over light at one end and light over darkness at the other, causing colors to appear. If the opportunity arises, look through a prism yourself. You will not find color if there is only light; only where darkness and light meet in a certain way. This is important and so basic, yet currently not taught, known or understood by most scientists and color-workers.

The result was that color had become more to Goethe than just "split up light". Goethe grasped that the darkness that we usually consider to be "nothing" actually is something, and that darkness is essential, not just to birth colors, but to birth life.

He found the essence of colors to be a vital and constructive force of nature. He even started to give colors characters and qualities. E.g he labeled Yellow with "intellect" and "good"...

The founder of the Anthroposophical (Greek: wisdom of man) Movement, **Rudolf Steiner** (1861-1925), revised and commented on Goethe's scripts, presenting his understanding of the knowledge of the essence of colors as part of his extensive publications. At the Goetheanum, an anthroposophical centre in Switzerland founded by Rudolf Steiner, besides many other subjects being taught, lectures are given on Goethe's color teachings, as well as at other anthroposophical schools and centres worldwide.

The Indian-born **Dinshah Ghadiali** (1873-1966) developed the Spectro-Chrome-Therapy, a clever but simple system which suggests selected colors for specific parts of the body which have typical symptoms of disease. Using his *"Twelve Color System"*, he had, to the joy of his often terminally ill patients, the most incredible successes. Unfortunately, the American Health Authorities and Medical Associations (he spent most of his life in America) were alarmed by his work and he was repeatedly accused of fraud and swindling by these institutions, as the newly developing pharmaceutical industry perceived him and his Spectro-Chrome-Therapy as competition and as a great threat that could ruin their newly developing grip on the marketplace. Meanwhile, many more openminded and less power hungry medical colleagues practised his system with the same success. They also used it in hospitals. As far as the Medical Associations and especially the pharmaceutical industry were concerned, his success spoke against him.

Like so many other great spirits, he was not permitted an easy life. His work was ahead of his time and the existing systems and their representatives were unable to grant this new system of healing its rightful place due to basic stupidity, shortsightedness, envy, greed and hunger for power, control and domination. Instead, his institutions were burnt down more than once, which resulted in the loss of many years of research work. He was sentenced to imprisonment and he had to pay great fines. His books, scripts and publications were banned and as a final sentence, he was even not allowed to receive his mail!

He was always accused of the same thing: the impossibility of his insistence that he had improved the health situation of his clients with colored light. To his accusers *"colored light"* was synonymous with *"nothing!"* Thus he was accused of swindling, as in their eyes he claimed to heal with nothing...

Dinshah Ghadiali took this calmly and continued to make his findings public. By then these conclusions had been proved and positively tested. However, they were still not acknowledged by any official body due to fear of pending consequences, or maybe less business for the drug companies?!

He was a very spiritual and intuitive man as well as a serious scientist, who developed his theories from a different basis (vedic) than his more conventional western colleagues. All these characteristics assisted him in his genius as an inventor. Despite all attempts to quieten him, his system is still popular today, inspiring many to deepen their understanding of color effects on the body/organs. Conventional science still does not understand the use of the power of the visible part of the electromagnetic spectrum, whereas people with a more holistic thinking approach use it in specialised and successful ways.

Personally, I can confirm the effect of color-light radiation from my own experience! I had not anticipated the enormous effect of color-light treatments and had at first underestimated the power of colors.

Despite the immense scientific and healing possibilities, it must be said that little attention has been given to color. The vast potential of the effects of colors in terms of their energetic and therapeutic potential remains largely untapped.

During the past sixty years mankind has made effective use of basic light colors (red, green, blue; RGB) for the development of color screens, monitors and television. Color photography and color film was developed and improved. Color printing techniques and process were refined and are now even available as computer printers at incredibly high quality at relatively low price for home and office use.

A few companies devote some effort to the choice of colors used on furnishings and machines for psychological reasons. Of course colors are being extensively applied in marketing and advertising. However, serious and extensive research into the essence of colors and their effects remains unrealised and research that has been done is waiting for mainstream acknowledgement.

In which ways does colored light change the biological-chemical structure? How do cell structures and microbes behave if exposed to colored light? Little consideration has been given to complementary colors and the effect of the after-image to the eye. What is color quality? These are all questions which to date cannot be answered in detail.

Personal Change Color Exercises

Throughout the book you will be provided with simple *personal change color exercise*. These techniques can help you change your perceptions about life, people and problems and can help you change your life. So give them a go because each exercise only takes a few minutes.

Here is the first one to start you off:

Personal Change Color Exercise: A Brighter Future!

The following exercise will help you brighten up your future. It utilises the power of color and visualisation to create a sense of optimism.

1. Imagine your future spreading out in front of you; Some people see a path extending out in front of them, others see a series of images leading off in front of them. *If you could imagine seeing your future, what would that look like now?*

2. Now, as you look at that representation of your future, imagine brightening up the vision by increasing the intensity of the colors in the image.

3. 3. What happens if you allow your favourite optimistic color (*gold?*) to spread and shine throughout that future representation. Simply imagine spreading that color throughout your future. *What is that like?*

Theophilus Heliodor Gimbel (1920- 2004) has founded "The Hygeia College of Color Therapy", based on many years of research in a small village in Gloucestershire in England, which sadly folded after his death. In his college the extensive spectrum of colors and its related natural laws in connection with the human being in accordance with his spiritual background and deep experience were lectured on.

His work is based on a healthy, realistic and practical spiritual understanding of the human, and has the following main aspects:

- Spiritual aspects for therapeutical work and especially for therapeutic work incorporating color and light

- Color and complementary color

- Shape and complementary shape

- The interplay and effect of color, shape and rhythm

- Color diagnosis via the spine

- Color therapy treatments

- Color visualisation, chakras and the aura

- Color therapy instruments

- llumination – quality of light and the effect on humans

- The use of color for decoration and clothing

- The effect of color and light on human and botanic cells...

Theo Gimbel taught that every human being can develop an ethical feeling and understanding from the knowledge and experience of natural laws and cosmic principles. He also advised that this should be part of the education of every person who is in a position of power, or has access to laboratories. This forms a criteria which hopefully will be reconsidered in the not too distant future. If we as a society and mankind really want to make progress, this truth is also a necessity in the school system.

A Pioneer of Color Psychology is Swiss born **Max Lüscher** (born 1923). His simple but finely detailed tests analyse the current psychological state of a personality through the attraction to or rejection of selected colors. He also discovered that the feeling towards different colors changes if their shape is altered (square, circle, triangle, pentagon etc.). This is to our mind an interesting subject, deserving further research and studies.

Max Lüscher's work also demonstrates another principle: a human being can only choose in accordance with his/her own condition i.e. an architect can only design houses reflecting himself. His ideas, his beliefs and ideology, his preferences but also his faults and fears, will become apparent in his buildings. Furthermore, he will choose the color of the buildings he designs in accordance with his present condition. A balanced and healthy architect will see the "human being" in the occupant and will understand the nature of the human needs. He will design a building to cater for all the needs of the residents in a balanced way. His beliefs, his balance, will be expressed in the interior and exterior design.

A *"short sighted"*, profit-orientated architect, who is used to thinking just in terms of *"units"* and not people, will only be able to produce a building that reflects his personal horizon. The result might well be a grey estate lacking any social or human aspect, ugly to look at with an accordant effect on its residents: a place of minor communication and high suicide and crime rate. In such a case one can say, a neurosis bears fruit.

This reality can only be corrected through a healthy frame of mind and there are signposts that this urgency is now creating the start of a new direction. The human being must start to heal his/her own mind in order to progress. Each product can only be as good, healthy and in balance as its designer. This even applies in a moral ethical sense.

For some time now various people and associations have studied and made use of colors. Together with psychics, vibration and aura sensing people, mental color projection is used to support curative processes. Once again we point out that the enormous effect of mental projection with intent should not be underestimated! Just because we are not used to utilizing this facility, does not mean it may not be the greatest power we as humans posses...!

In the early 1980s, a research team of scientists revealed certain physical characteristics that are essential for the effectiveness of light therapy and created a light source that was originally based on low-level laser therapy but actually worked with almost the whole range of visible light and a portion of infrared light. Based on this technology the Bioptron Light & Color Therapy System was created.

Bioptron Light Therapy has become accepted as a new form of treatment in prevention, therapy and rehabilitation. Bioptron in Switzerland is working continuously with experts, researchers and physicians in many countries in order to examine the characteristics and therapeutic effectiveness of Bioptron Light Therapy. The basic machines for this non-pharmaceutical therapy are not that expensive and can be used in the home as wall as in clinics. Bioptron offers not just light therapy but also color therapy devices, with color filters of the highest quality made from glass.

Lily Cornford founded "The Maitreya School Of Healing" in London, extensive and detailed mental color healing is practised and taught. Lily has investigated many different aspects of healing but her primary area of interest was in direct color healing – using her mind, her heart and her own hands.

Vicky Wall, who gave up her physical presence in 1991, was a chemist and developed, after becoming blind, a highly sophisticated color-oil-essences-system called "Aurasoma". Her oils and essences are charged with energies of various realms, e.g. crystals, herbs, homeopathy,..., which she was able to sense in great detail. With this ability, plus her strong intuition and her knowledge as a chemist, she developed this beautiful and lovely smelling color-system, which is now available from trained Aurasoma therapists, and is still an ongoing color teaching.

In order to provide a foundation and a representative body for the growing number of people interested in and working with color, in 1984 the "International Association of Color Therapists" (IACT) was founded in England now it is "The International Association of Color" (IAC). Even though most pioneering work in the field of color is still done in England, IAC has members in many countries all over the world, most of whom studied the subject in England. http://www.iac-color.co.uk

Personal Change Color Exercise: Rose Tinted Glasses

There is a common idiom in the English language; *"When someone is in love, they look at their partner through rose tinted glasses."* If you where to ask that person to describe their inner subjective experience you would discover that they actually color their internal image of their partner in a rose pink hue. This is one of the ways their mind codes their imagery so that they know, *"This is the person I love."*

We can use this knowledge to change our subjective experience of reality:

1. Think of something that you would like a new perspective on.

2. Select a resource that you would like to experience in the above. e.g.) Optimism, creativity, relaxation, happiness etc.

3. Represent that resource with a color.

4. Now imagine in front of you a pair of sunglasses which are colored with the color you selected in Step 3.

5. Put them on and look at the situation you selected in Step 1 with this new colored perspective.

6. Enjoy the new learnings you've gained. Perhaps try it again with other colored glasses.

7. Would it be useful to have those glasses on in future situations? Imagine a future situation, see what you would see and hear what you would hear as you imagine the situation through those colored shades...

But What Is Color?

Try to imagine that everything is one color. How would we recognise shapes? In order to recognise anything the human eye requires the specific color. In experiments to show the shapes in flowing water, colored water is introduced into clear water to distinguish the forms, and smoke is used in experiments to show the shape behaviour of air.

Color and shape are opposite poles, much like man and woman, left and right, inside and outside. In fact, in our brain, color is processed in the intuitive right side (*female*), and shape in the left side of the intellect (*male*). This shows us that we cannot truly understand the effect of colors with our intellect alone. In order to understand, and especially experience color, we must dive deep into the world of emotions, feelings and inner perceptions, the feminine side of our being.

In mainstream science, spiritual-scientific aspects, based on the intuitive and feminine part of ourselves, are not considered. This results in the neglect of the inner parts (*soul*) of human beings. Intuitive experiences are rejected as being only of the imagination. The spiritual teacher White Eagle teaches that imagination is an expression which is used in too loose a way. Imagination or visualisation, according to White Eagle, is the entrance into the truly spiritual realm. If natural science acknowledges the internal as a reality, it will be able to seriously experiment on the effect of colors. The question, *"but what is color?"*, can only be answered if we are guided by our personal sensitivity, learn to listen to our feelings and take them seriously.

The reason contemporary conventional science has not

spent much consideration on color and its effect is simple: Knowledge is divided into empirical science and spiritual science, which again are polarities. Color information is processed in the female, right part of the brain. Male, intellectual approaches stem from the left brain, and it is only these intellectual approaches which are cultivated and fostered in our universities and scientific institutions.

A few physical facts follow, continuing into a description of the various colors and their properties. However, true knowledge of the effect of colors can only be achieved by one's own experience:

- By developing sensitivity towards color

- By observing the internal feelings upon confrontation with various colors

- By experiments with colors and their complementary colors (e.g in paintings) – and noticing the different qualities of the colors; what inner pictures sensations they bring

- By specific observation of after images

- By observation of sunrise and sunset

- By the observation of personal life periods and the relevant color requirements

- By the observation of colors within nature and contemplating their expressive purpose, by asking the color, *"what do you do to me?"*

I invite you to trust your feelings. Trust yourself, every day a bit more. What you find out for yourself is your personal knowledge and, for you, right! No external authority can give you self-confidence. You can request and receive external confirmation, but self-confidence, your internal authority, can only come from you. I encourage you to give respect, weight and authority to what you perceive inwardly. It is true in you. We all know our inner perceptions change with time. But at each time they are the truth we live with. Our schools have not encouraged and skilled us to listen to our inner voices, and to value their messages.

To become more whole this is something worth catching up on. In the Findhorn Foundation Community in Scotland, workshops are held which in part encourage *inner listening*. Or through playing the intuitive PANGARDEN Game from Findhorn (see Resources). While Pangarden helps to transform real life issues, you also, in a playful way, learn to trust your intuition more. This new game is based on trusting yourself to intuitively find the next step in the game from the options provided. Unlike usually, where a dice is *"consulted,"* Pangarden also contains a number of 12 different colored mats in three archetypical shapes to help you lay out the constellation of your situation, thus holistically accessing the different brain sides through color and shape.

Everyone, as an individual, has specific requirements in accordance with his/her specific rhythm. Only you can be in contact and harmony with your own rhythm, your own universe. Harmony with the external universe follows automatically. Self-confidence in your own judgment, recognition and consideration of your immense internal potentials, are the first steps to decrease external authority and increase internal authority.

This acknowledgement of your own individual personality and the resulting authority towards yourself can produce wonderful results. An additional invitation is to accept the variations in personalities and rhythms and timing in people around us. Many people already accept this, but soon we all will have to address this more fully as the global population has increased by threefold over the last 50 years. In many ways we have, as a society, become more recluse, as individuals insulated behind our screens and in a way *"autistic"*. Yet the challenge is there to engage with others more and learn to tolerate the other. Not so easy it seems, if we look at the high divorce rate and how many people are single and/or struggling in relationships. Sensing colors consciously can support these processes of learning to experience and tolerate the other...

Indeed we are very close to recognising the effect of colors on a larger scale if the personal judgment within the individual human being develops self-confidence in its own *"right"* yet has the flexibility to forgive, tolerate and embrace the other.

Personal Change Color Exercise: Word Magic

The phrases that fly out of our mouths sometimes contain real magic that we can use to our benefit. Have you ever heard phrases such as:

1. *"I saw it/him/her in a new light."*

2. *"You have a bright future ahead of you."*

3. *"The opportunity is golden!"*

4. *"She had a kind of spiritual aura about her; electric*

blue/white"

These phrases are Neuro-Linguistic processes, meaning the person's internal imagery is actually colored with what the words say. e.g.) *"The opportunity is golden!"* We can use this process to change our perceptions in a useful way:

Seeing People in a New Light

1. Think about an experience when you "saw someone in a new light."

2. Notice in your mind's eye what color that new light was.

3. Now think about someone currently in your life that you would benefit from seeing in a new light.

4. Imagine them in your mind and then see them in the new light. That is imagine them within the new light color.

5. 5. Notice how this changes your perception of that person. And become aware of any new learnings.

Electromagnetic Spectrum Diagram

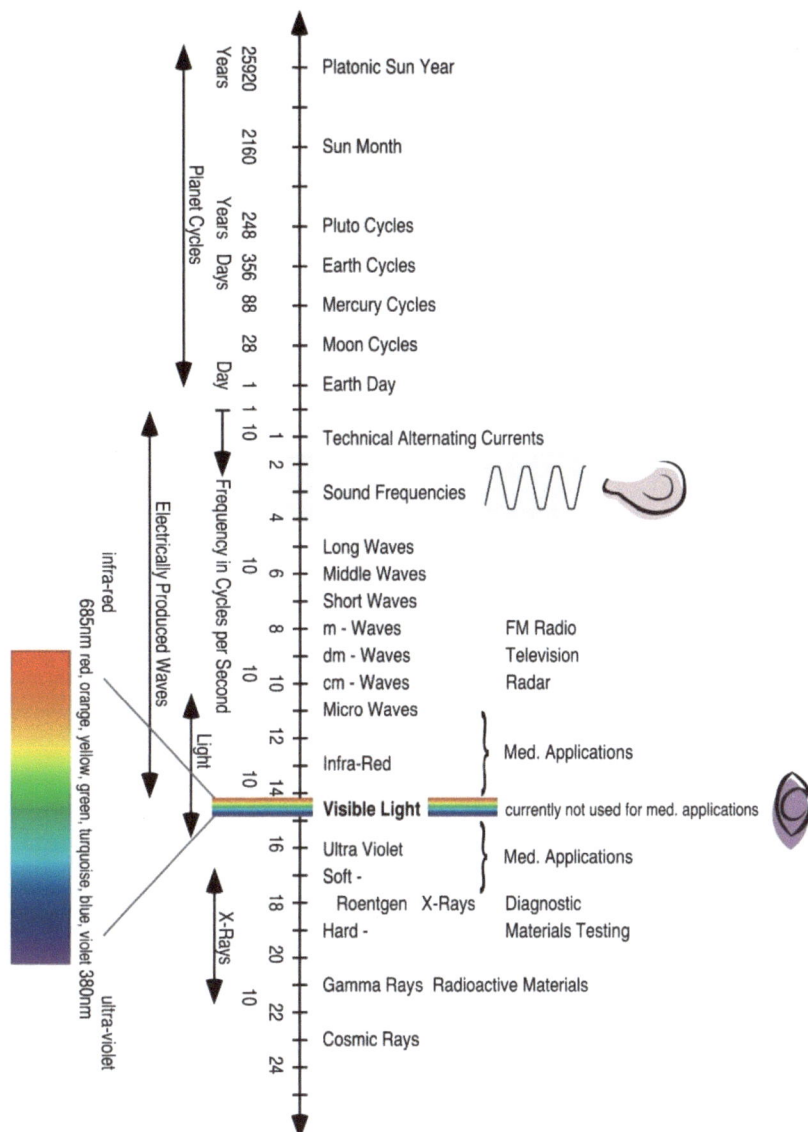

Magenta Spiral Diagram

Note: Magenta appears only in the spiral presentation (not in the scientific/linear presentation above!)

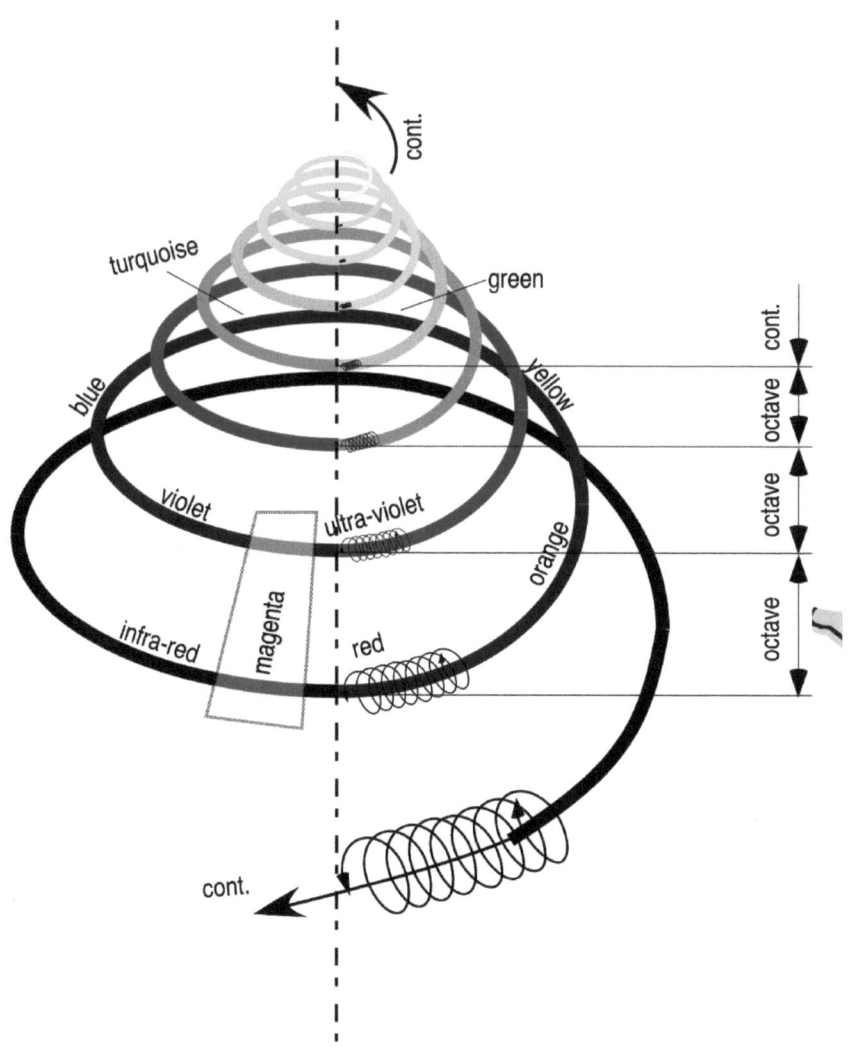

General Comments about Color and Light

Colors surround us. Everything has its own unique color. We are used to colors. Because of this familiarity we often do not attribute much importance to color. If we look at the Electromagnetic Spectrum on the next page, we find that color and light – the visible part of the spectrum for the human being – is positioned between ultra-violet and infra-red light.

Infra-red, for example, has a warming effect on the human body and is used in curative medical applications. Ultra-violet has a tanning effect. Latest experiments show that a deficiency of ultra-violet light, especially in winter, can result in Vitamin D deficiency which creates all sorts of imbalances in the body, not just depression. As far as the effect of the other parts of the spectrum on the human being are concerned, we have less information. We know for example of the effect of extreme doses of X-rays or radioactivity. As with everything, the effect of electromagnetic vibration is dependent on the dosage. In any case, in physical terms, color and light are energy and thus do have an effect! Dr Lieberman states, *"Light and health are inseparable."*

Color is energy and as such directly effects the human cell. This is the true effect of color! Even mental color projection is energy since we know that thoughts create streams which we can actually measure. The effects of colors are proven. Maybe you thought up to now that the effect of colors is only created by your sub-conscious? Now you can perhaps begin to realise their effect to be far more profound and far reaching, and have a physically proven foundation.

Color influences the condition of the cells within the body and therefore also the condition of the consciousness. Blind people show the same reaction to colors as people with eyesight and some blind people can *"see"* colors in their own way, which means they can feel the power of the electromagnetic frequency – the vibration of what we call color. A person with eyesight can also achieve this ability, it is just a matter of sensitivity and training. To quote Dr Lieberman again, *"There is more to vision than meets the eye."* We are so used to the experience of perceiving color on a day-to-day level that we do not actually consciously realise the impact it has on our system.

One frequently asked question is whether colors have the same effect on everybody or whether this effect varies. In fact, both are true. Even if the effect of the color is always the same, the reaction to it differs widely depending on the condition of each individual.

Let us use cake as an example in order to exemplify the effects of color. Cake will always pass through the same process after being eaten: stomach, stomach acid, digestion, blood circulation... etc. This is the natural path of a piece of cake when eaten. However, viewed individually, it can mean sustenance for the hungry, joy and encouragement to the sad, and for somebody who has already eaten 4 pieces, it might mean that this same piece of cake will result in sickness and vomiting. The same piece of cake can bring variety into a life used to, *"warmed up stew"*. Someone with a low level of blood sugar will react differently to this piece of cake than someone with a high level of blood sugar or even diabetes.

We view the individual reaction to a piece of cake, dependent on the requirement and condition of an individual. The cake remains the same. This principle applies to colors too.

We are individually different, and as a response to the internal question, *"which color is now good for me, which color do I need the most today for a healthy balance?"*, I will now receive a different answer from when I ask the same question tomorrow. For yourself, you will receive a different answer to mine. This shows that we are permanently moving and changing beings, that we have different requirements and needs at different times in order to keep us in a healthy balance.

Only our internal judgment, the personal internal authority, the silent internal voice, can tell us what is best for us today, and in what measure. What I require today is something only I and no outside authority can judge. Due to this we require the development of an internal authority as well as all the mentioned internal qualities if we want to be *"healthy"* – here seen in the wider sense. The current state of our planet and its inhabitants show that this fact has been neglected. This proves that we must extend our horizon, that we require something *"healthier."*

I would like to point out a principle which unfortunately has been more or less forgotten, however it is now being reconsidered step-by-step by many. If the human being gets out of balance the symptoms of this imbalance will by their nature force the personality to look at its causes. Considered in this way, a human being as a whole will always be *"healthy."* Our body may well make use of challenging physical symptoms to cleanse or release physical, emotional, mental or spiritual conditions. Illness is therefore more a friend to be listened to than an enemy to be fought. We usually have to create a new balance to regain certain functions. Within that, so long as we are on Earth, we have to learn and change, and our body is one of our teachers. Creating the right balance to function well is our challenge.

The task of a proper therapist or a responsible doctor is to recognise the imbalance and to activate and support the recovery process using suitable means, creating a new balance.

It is a mistaken fact of our times that illness is treated only as an enemy to be fought. Illness in fact is our best teacher, showing us that we have lost contact with ourselves, our real nature, our balance, and furthermore enabling us, through the symptoms, to get back onto the right path. For the soul, illness is a natural and healing balancer. C.G. Jung describes this principle by stating that a neurosis appears as a messenger, saying that a change of attitude of the self is needed. The neurosis can heal us, rather than us healing the neurosis...

Personal Change Color Exercise: Color Polarity Exercise

This exercise enables you to gain new perspectives on problems or stuck states of mind by representing the problem as a color and shape. You are then asked to represent the polar opposite of that with a new color and shape. Finally you combine these two polar opposites together which enables the mind to come up with new perspectives and insights into the problem.

1. Notice where in your body you feel the problem or stuck state.

2. If you were to give it a shape and color what would that be like?

---

3. Set that aside for a moment and now think about what the opposite of that state is. e.g.) The opposite of feeling stuck could be flying free.

4. What shape and color is the opposite state?

5. Now imagine perceiving the shapes and colors of the two states together at the same time.

6. How quickly or slowly can you allow those to two states to merge together into a new shape and color?

7. Looking at that new shape and color, notice how your experience has changed.

8. Think about the original problem and notice new changes, perspectives or insights.

After Image, Complementary Color and Octave

If we look for approximately 20 seconds in a relaxed way at a surface of red color and afterwards direct our eyes to a white surface, soon the "after image" will be visible to us.

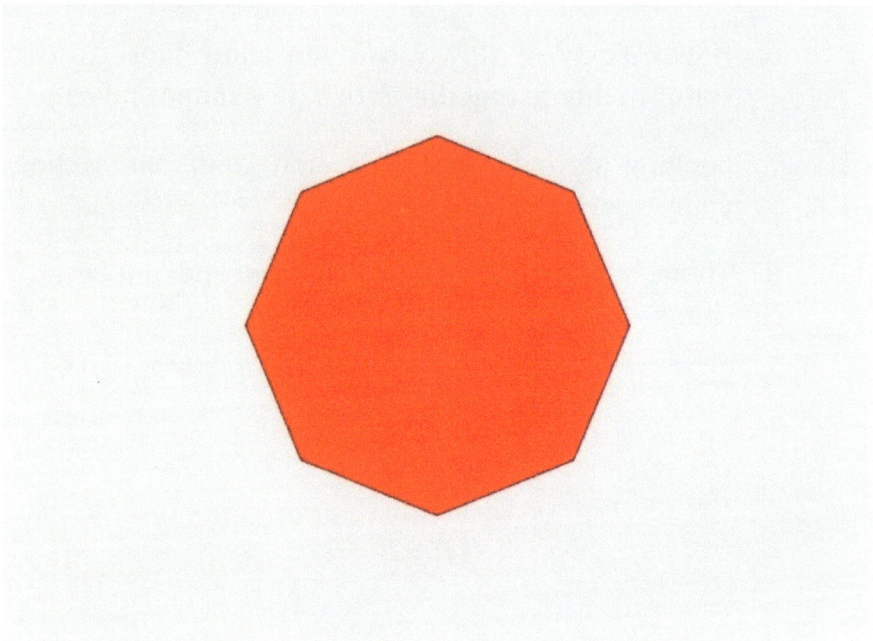

The viewed blank surface will show the shape in the complementary color, in this case a bright turquoise blue. This after image disappears after a period of time or as our consciousness is diverted by thoughts. In this way we can determine and experience complementary colors. The complimentary color after image, in a certain way, shows the impact a color made onto the eye and related nerves and senses.

The power of complementary colors and the internally perceived afterimages have been researched by Goethe, Steiner and Gimbel. After extensive color and light research on how to keep the human eye flexible and responsive, the pioneering, simple but effective Hygeia Eye-Strengthening Chart was developed by the late Theophilus Heliodor Gimbel. The Eye-Strengthening Chart benefits result from offering maximum exercise to the eye and related inner senses! Besides after image and shape, this fascinating chart also utilises the fact that the eye focuses far away when we look at blue, and on close up when we look at red...(see Resources for details.)

The complementary colors stand as follows:

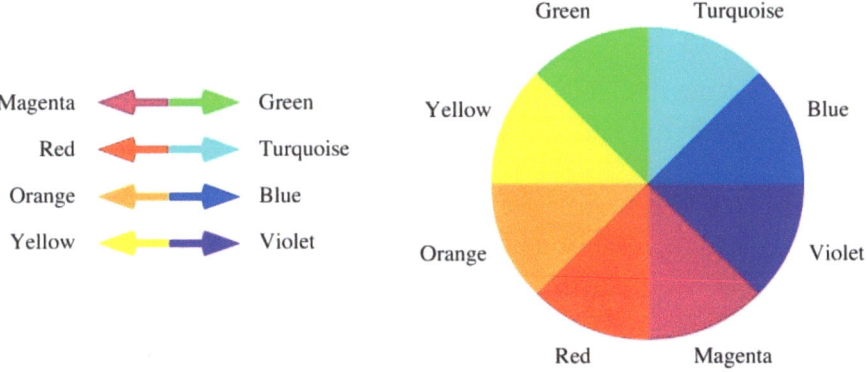

As the colors blend into each other, we can show them as a circle with the complementary colors positioned opposite.

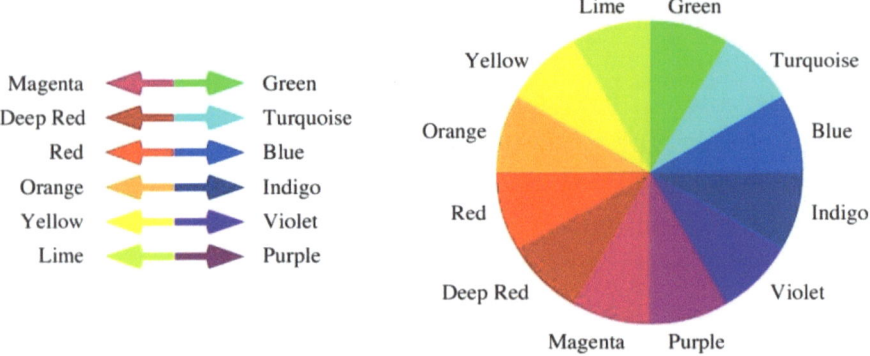

Magenta ←——→ Green
Deep Red ←——→ Turquoise
Red ←——→ Blue
Orange ←——→ Indigo
Yellow ←——→ Violet
Lime ←——→ Purple

If we now remember the diagram of electromagnetic vibrations, the visible spectrum moves on both sides into the invisible spectrum. For this the color circle is an aid and in reality it has the form of a spiral.

The human eye is able to see one turn of the spiral – one octave. To use a circle as a helpful and easily understood tool seems appropriate, but please remember that in fact it is a spiral which becomes visible at magenta and moves on to the next level also at magenta. In science color is displayed in a linear way as in the diagram of the Electromagnetic Spectrum. Due to this, magenta, where the ends of the visible spectrum meet in the spiral, is never shown. Consider nature, where the spiral is the motivating force within. Trees often arrange their branches in the pattern of a spiral, particles falling in a vacuum can be observed descending in a spiral and not straight. Our DNA has a spiral shape, our entire living universe is one huge spiral and if we go further into detail we realise that the spiral is the representative of each living and growing part of nature (implosion – spiral – to create, rather than explosion – linear – to destroy). The principle of the octave is a principle we can find again and again in our universe, if we have learned to recognise it. We have found eight colors through our experiments. Eight = Octave.

Red – Orange – Yellow – Green – Turquoise – Blue – Violet – Magenta.

Of course we can divide these eight colors further, and this will result, also as in music, in a unit of twelve to which we are very related. This twelvefoldness was for example used by Dinshah Ghadiali:

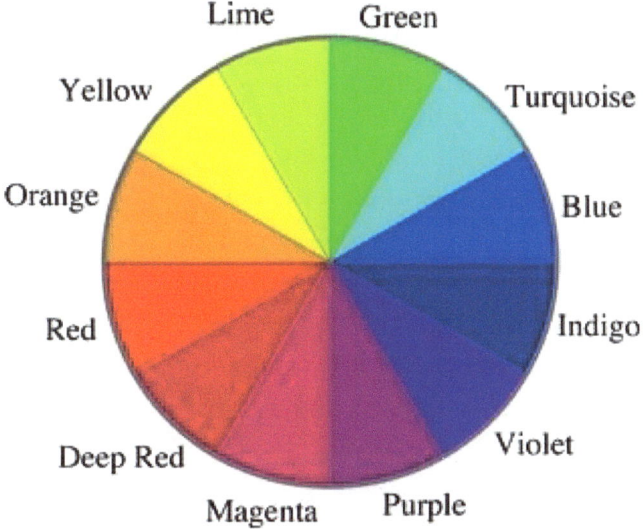

We could subdivide these colors further and further, but we would only achieve shades of the eight original colors.

Colors can have a wide spectrum or a small/narrow spectrum. Green with a wide spectrum ranges from yellow to turquoise and we can see that by closer observation. These wide spectrum colors can be found in nature, i.e. in flowers petals and leaves of plants, in minerals, in the colors of the heavens during sunrise and sunset,... These wide spectrum colors are the eight main colors of the spectrum. And there are colors to show part of the spectrum of one color only. These have a low bandwidth and show a specific, narrow frequency.

The shade of a color is the result of the light and darkness factor of the color and its position in the spectrum. So each color can be produced in virtually endless nuances, depending on its light and darkness factor, on the position in the spectrum and on the width of spectrum and the mixture of colors.

On the website we specifically set up for this book www.effective-color.com you can click on the colors to see some wide spectrum images, e.g. an orange that gradates from red all the way to yellow. For example rose petals often show colors with a wide spectrum, i.e. orange with a hint of red and a hint of yellow – on the same place without gradation. Good stain glass also has a wide spectrum – often made with special and expensive ingredients like gold or copper compounds. E.G in a good yellow you can detect a hint of green, yet also a hint of orange. This means a wide spectrum color spans from one end of its color spectrum right to the other side. Quite amazing to see when one has the opportunity - look closely at the color of rose and other flower petals to find these wide spectrum colors.

In physics, red, yellow and blue are considered the basic pigment colors as all other colors result from these if mixed. However, color printing techniques using CMYK C=Cyan, M=Magenta, Y=Yellow, K=Key color (=black) are found to produce the best results and are commonly used in industry for all kinds of printing; like newspapers, magazines, packaging, advertising,... On newspapers one can usually find at the bottom or some other area near the edge a small section where the four CMYK colors are being applied for test and quality control purposes in their original ink color.

Colored light has the basic colors red, green and blue. TV and computer monitors have three color leads RGB (Red,

Green, Blue).

And did you know that colored lights can create beautiful colored shades if two or more colored lights are used?! Theo Gimbel in his Hygeia Studios research lab had a big screen onto which colors and colored shadows were projected from behind in a rhythmical way. It was an amazingly soothing experience, and he suggested it for trauma recovery. I feel a smaller machine like that would work well in homes as it has something harmonising, aesthetically interesting and pleasing.

The complementary color has an important role! Being the biggest possible opposite pole it gives the color the best effect. The biggest difference and tension is found between poles and each pole only becomes such through its opposite. Only by having an opposite pole does the pole becomes alive and forceful. This polarisation of colors has furthermore the advantage that the opposite pole acts as equaliser. In color therapy it is advised to utilise the complementary color in a smaller proportion as well.

Opposite poles belong to each other as they have something in common:

Red – Turquoise	i.e. Hot – Cold
Orange – Blue	i.e. Extrovert – Introvert
Yellow – Violet	i.e. Independent – Safely Guided
Green – Magenta	i.e. Stability – Change

These examples can not cover the entire connection between opposite poles and are only mentioned to show you that the one cannot exist without the other, indeed creates the other (colors included), and to encourage you to think further.

Personal Change Color Exercise: Color Wheel Exercise

You'll have seen the color wheel, on the next page, earlier in the book. Or you can go here to see a full screen version: http://www.effective-color.com

By allowing your eyes to gaze at a certain color, on the wheel, you will help to balance your overall Physical, Emotional, Mental and Spiritual (PEMS) levels.

A more advanced way of using the Color Wheel is to do the above exercise first and then hold an issue/problem you want to address in your mind while you allow your eyes to go to a color they feel drawn too. This way you give your system some overall balance first and then from that balance you get more input for a specific issue/problem.

Color Wheel (go here for a more detailed Color Wheel ==> **http://www.effective-color.com**)

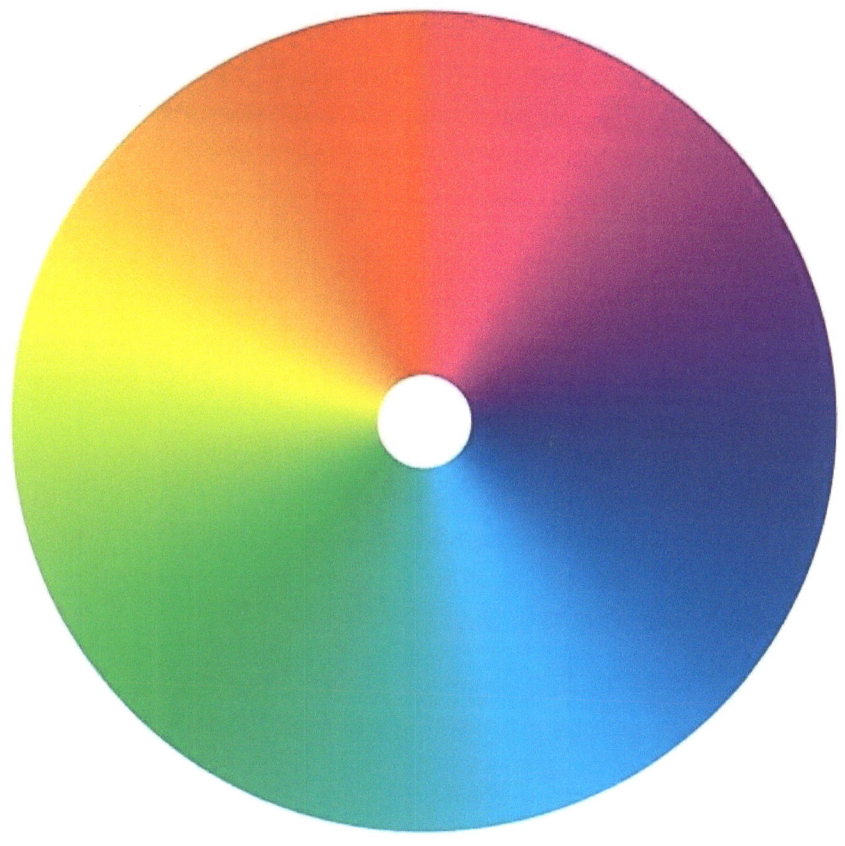

A Few Words About Chakras

The Sanskrit word "chakra" means "wheel". Chakras are referred to as flowers and spinning energy-vortices also called energy-centres. These energy centres are in the subtle body surrounding our physical one. Psychically developed and sensitive people are much more aware of this reality than our science is able to prove.

We have seven major chakras, which have their physical counterparts in the endocrine system. Physically they are seen as colored and correlate to the organs in the body where they are positioned.

If the energy centre is out of balance, the corresponding organs will be affected. Disease starts in the energy fields around the body via negative thoughts and emotions, e.g. fear, rigidity, greed, cruelty,..., gradually permeating and manifesting in the physical.

Qualities seen in the chakras and in the energy field reflect the qualities of the person's character, spiritual development, etc. Independent of this, chakras can be "open" and "closed"!

"Open" in this context means the capacity to act as a doorway or window for mediating forces. This is the reason why a great deal of attention is put on the discipline aspect of meditation before "opening up". To avoid unwanted influences penetrating, it is suggested to first feel comfortably centred and then to surround oneself mentally with positive light and ask the Great Spirit, or God one believes in and relates to, to be present.

At the end of a meditation or healing it is vital to "close

down" again. This can be done by visualising the chakras one by one, starting at the top, like a flower closing. Finally you should also surround yourself with an energy field of light.

Mental commands affect the subtle bodies very quickly. Thoughts are indeed energies which can be consciously directed. It is only in recent centuries that "ideas" have been seen as abstract and intellectually rooted. In Plato's time the word "idea" meant a living form which resided in the spiritual realm!

To give a simplistic explanation of each chakra:

1) **The Root-Chakra** is red and connected with all "Red" and "Mars" matters. Its location is between the legs at the base of the spine. It contains the primal energies, which in our "civilised world" we shy away from or get obsessed by. Particularly in woman, anger and spontaneity can be repressed due to conditioning, resulting in low body temperature – cold "extremities" - and maybe challenging external relationships. Feeling good about initiating things, one's sexuality and the "will" is necessary.

2) **The Splenic-Chakra** is orange, associated with "Venus matters" and is located underneath the navel. This rules joy, pleasure, creativity, social activity. Also rules digestive processes in the main, as well as gut reactions and feelings.

3) **The Solar-Plexus-Chakra** is yellow and as the communication centre is seen in connection with Mercury, receiving and transmitting messages from lower to higher centres and vice versa, and to the outer world. This is the chakra we automatically protect with our hands when in a situation of discomfort or stress.

4) **The Heart-Chakra** is seen as green and connected with the energies of the sun and of Neptune. It is the centre where we can love compassionately and should not erect barriers. This links in with the Christ-consciousness and is the middle chakra in the body. It weighs up the personal and the spiritual.

5) **The pale blue Throat-Chakra** is associated with the energies of Jupiter. It is the centre of sound and its formative, creative power. It is also the centre connected with our inner and outer authority.

6) **The Third-Eye-Chakra** is dark blue, on the forehead and connected with the planet Pluto. It rules the inner seeing and clairvoyance, conscious mental projection and thus creation power, an ability which is very latent in the people of today.

7) **The Crown-Chakra** on the top of the head is violet and is linked with Uranus. This is our connection to the Cosmos, just as red, the Base, is our connection to the Earth. They are equally important in showing us that we are inhabitants of both the Spiritual World and the planet Earth. It is important not to just develop higher "spiritual" centres, but also the others, lest the latter confront us with feelings/experiences we try to ignore. Sexuality, fun and day to day life are good foundations for our development and are great teachers!

Color Energy Chakra Balancing Meditation

The following chakra meditation will help you balance your chakra energy system by imagining each chakra's color in turn starting with the color red at the root chakra and then working up through the other chakra's.

1. Find a comfortable position either sitting or laying down. Take a few deep clearing breaths and begin breathing slowly and evenly.

2. Visualise a golden light above your head and draw the light all the way down your body to your feet.

3. Imagine the light illuminating every part of your being.

4. As you allow yourself to become more and more relaxed, you can begin meditating on each chakra, starting with the Root Chakra. Meditate on the chakra's location, color and attributes as you work your way up each one to the Crown Chakra:

    • Root Chakra = Red; Base of the spine

    • Splenic Chakra = Orange; Underneath the navel

    • Solar Plexus Chakra = Yellow; Solar Plexus

- The Heart Chakra = Green; Heart Centre

- The Throat Chakra = Pale Blue; Throat

- The Third Eye Chakra = Dark Blue; In-between Eyes

- The Crown Chakra = Violet; Top of Head

5. Closing the meditation properly is done by visualising the chakras one by one, starting at the top, closing like a flower. Finish your meditation by taking a few more deep breaths and imagine golden light filling your entire being from above.

The Effects of Colors

The following is meant only to be an aid to your own experiences with colors and should not replace these. I hope you will find these summaries supportive and encouraging.

These descriptions of the effects of colors are not, and cannot be, complete and I would like to point out that in these days of quick change the human being will change too. This will lead to changes in the effect of colors.

As we become more sensitive, these changes will become apparent to us and we will have to be prepared to exchange our old theories for new realities, a task which we will have to meet in many aspects of life.

Red

Red is activating, encouraging an increase of blood pressure and awakening the sleepy. It can drive the already overactive frenetic. Red as a therapy color must be used very carefully due to its stimulating characteristics.

Red activates us, it is force and dynamics, anger and aggression. Red means attention, red is the fright. Red increases heart activity, pulse, breathing and also the eyelid movement, all signs of terror, internal awareness and physical readiness.

But red is love as well. Red has a wide spectrum. In combination with black it shows the aspects of anger, impatience, rage, brutality and cruelty. Combined with pink, red shows the gentle power of love and emotional tenderness.

A reddened part of flesh, an irritation on the body is already a trouble spot. Inflamed processes become worse if exposed to the color red. The complementary color turquoise or blue should be used in therapy. An inflammation of the tonsils will be more difficult to cure if a red scarf is worn! An aching head or migraine will be relaxed if a turquoise head-dress is worn.

Lethargic people, those with problems facing daily routine, will find this easier if they are surrounded by some red; a picture, a table cloth, a red glass, red flowers – why not red underwear from time to time? Some therapists recommend red to women in order to encourage conception. Red is the color of blood, of our physical existence and it is the color of the Base-Chakra.

Red is placed in close connection to our sexuality, reproduction, our animal instincts, our ability to survive the daily routine and its conflicts, our physical energy, our ego and our instinct to survive. Seen from an astrological- mythological angle, red is our Mars energy.

This red energy is the energy of a warrior and an initiator, the energy to express our individuality. A difficult situation for many is how to be "nice" and to make it "right for everyone". A little aid from the color red helps us to make ourselves occasionally heard and seen and to make space for our own wishes and requirements! Studies show that many cancer patients belong to the most friendly and tolerant patients and that they are also the most passive. During cancer treatment one should not only think of the cancer cells, but also of the suppressed individuality.

We can also meet suppressed red "Mars" energy from the outside in the form of terror and in that case we are "the innocent victim", having to learn to deal with this form of energy in that way.

Once again it must be said that the color red must be treated carefully. One should not use red excessively and bright red walls should be avoided. Some carefully chosen objects will achieve the required success. Too much will result in an over activation of the senses and of the nervous system and the result will be a general irritation and an increased danger of inflammation. This will then result in tiredness and exhaustion.

A red environment gives the subjective feeling that time passes more quickly (used in fast food restaurants to achieve quicker turnover) and it will make the environment appear smaller which can result in claustrophobic experiences.

As mentioned before, during color therapy in general, complementary colors should also be used in order to provide the natural opposite pole, which will in turn improve the color effect but also provide a healthy balance.

Orange

Orange is stimulating, too, but it stimulates not only the body (although not as much as red) but the mind as well. It activates in a more playful way, with more joy and creativity. Orange is not as strong and not as stubborn as red.

Orange is social, joyful and anti-depressive. It brings, like red, the consciousness down to earth, into the so called reality and the present, but this happens in a joyful fashion.

One organises with joy, plans with joy and plays with joy. One looks upon life in a positive way. Orange is "the playing child". It plays with concentration and joy, not too concentrated on the aim, the play itself is more important to the child. Red is more serious, forced and even sacrifices others whereas for orange, the aim is not so important and more emphasis is placed on the game being fun. Orange develops creativity and joyful play in the adult. It supports the connection back to personal feelings (2nd Chakra).

A theory worth mentioning has demonstrated that orange stands via octaves in resonance connection with the human DNA, which means that what a human being is and wishes to be is easier to achieve with orange. Interesting is the fact that the students of Buddhism, the Sanjassin, wear orange clothing. But it must be mentioned at this point that too much orange will result in lethargy and a passive attitude, it weakens ones own will and subjects one to manipulation.

Orange as the color of the 2nd Chakra is the color of digestion. It reminds us that eating should be a social act of joy. Studies show that people eating in community, are on average healthier than people eating alone. Fast food chains and others have recognised the connection between orange and food as well as its stimulating effect on the human being. They exploit this in combination with other inviting colors.

During the past decades, many cheap, one-use and throw-away products mainly made from plastic, were produced in bright orange. Unfortunately due to this, orange is too often associated with cheap rubbish and is therefore resented. However, orange is a very good and freshening color for the human being and one should consider this fact when furnishing a dining room. But once again it must not be used excessively.

Yellow

Yellow is the brightest color next to light and is therefore often associated with light. Yellow takes one "up". Yellow is the color of the sun, the intellect, the distance, the detachment, the easiness and the cheerfulness.

As the color of the intellect, thoughts, new ideas and the left part of the brain, it is connected to mental work and logical thinking. Yellow pushes the consciousness upwards, from where one has a better view and from this personal distance matters are dealt with in a more objective way. An assumption for positive criticism and analysis. Yellow is also the color of the inventor; of originality and change.

Yellow is the color of spring and future. Human beings have a craving for yellow if they have passed an internal process and are now prepared to release emotional nostalgic feelings. After this internal "spring cleaning" a lot of old pressure is released and the newly achieved internal easiness represents an internal spring. Then yellow is like fresh air in which breathing is easy and relaxed.

Wearing yellow clothing is not to everyone's taste. This is not so much due to the color but because of the inhibiting feeling of being watched and seen and at the same time feeling alone and isolated. It is a good color to consider everything with distance, to have the peace to enjoy or rebuild the internal existence. Human beings able to "be on their own" show a particular liking towards yellow clothing. In schizophrenia, these distanced and separated feelings have reached their unhealthy extreme.

Due to its distancing effect, yellow is the worst color to be used in mental institutions. Also, people working too much with their logical mind, who risk losing the connection to their feelings and intuition, should eliminate yellow from their lives for a certain amount of time. (This applies to the color yellow in food, too).

The isolating effect of having a skin as well as the possibility of communication beyond the border of skin are characteristics of yellow and therefore yellow stands in close connection with the skin. Yellow is the color of the Solar-plexus-chakra and is mostly associated with Mercury the communicator, the messenger of the gods.

The Solar-plexus is the communicator between higher feelings and thoughts and the personal ego, forming the communication bridge for the emotional condition towards other human beings. As far as interior design and clothing is concerned, yellow is a brightening, fresh, happy and inspiring color and can therefore be recommended wherever these effects are required. It is good for lecture and study rooms.

Pale yellow shows a changeable analytical mind with much curiosity. Deep yellow reflects wisdom, as mentioned later in Gold.

Green

The color of the centre, the balance and the equaliser. The color green is focused directly on the retina in the eye. Red is focused behind the retina and blue in front of the retina. Red items seem to be closer than blue items even if these are of same size and distance.

Green as the color of the centre is also the color of the heart-chakra, the centre chakra. Our consciousness should be directed from our centre, from our heart, in balance with our personal and non-personal higher requirements.

Green is neither stimulating nor relaxing. It is static and equalises matters, and therefore puts them into balance. For example, cancer-cell growth can be reduced using green light under medical supervision, as shown by Theo Gimbel, England.

Green in the aura of a patient shows that his condition is stabilising and that therefore the first step towards recovery has been made. Green has a strong cleansing effect on the body and strengthens and stabilises the nervous system. A walk in the "green" enables the body to regenerate, and the mind and emotions can be balanced which is especially important for decision making.

Green is associated with immaturity, but also with success, hope and money.

Green is a balance point and very strong as such. Green plays an essential role in our lives! Balance, relaxation and harmony are essential for the health of the human being. This is the philosophy of the medical system of the old Chinese, which mainly focuses on preventative, balancing and harmonising treatments. This should be considered when we choose the colors for our environment and clothing. House plants can be highly supportive of our health.

Very dark green shades can have a depressive effect after some time. Too much green is regarded as boring and inflexible.

Turquoise

Balancing between green and blue, therefore between regenerating and relaxing.

Turquoise is best described as refreshing. Cool and refreshing like a shower on a hot summer day or like the ice of the North Pole. Turquoise-blue as the color of the throat-chakra is, especially with children, more the color of creativity, self expression and communication on a higher level than the base chakra (red). Pure turquoise is the color of the Thymus gland centre, an energy centre between the heart and throat chakras, though it is not as strong as the seven main chakras.

The Thymus gland plays a leading role within the immune system. However, the specific function within the adult is not yet known.

To be immune means not to take in everything, but to be consciously selective, to choose what is good for oneself and what is not, using the acknowledged good and to be "immune" against the rest. The throat-chakra is furthermore connected to internal authority, the authority with priority to oneself. Authority towards others follows automatically.

Turquoise as a cooling and refreshing color supports the healing of inflamed processes within the body and turquoise-blue relaxes an irritated nerve system.

Blue

Blue forms the largest part of daylight. Daylight incandescent lamps have blue tinted glass to live up to their name. Blue colored light is our natural environment. Healthy cell growth has the best basis if exposed to blue light.

Experiments with plants have shown that blue light influences the growth and flavour of plants in a positive way. Red light makes the shoots grow too fast and due to that the plants become spindly and the taste of plants becomes bad (sharp). Green light also restricts the growth of plants, as shown in experiments by Theo Gimbel, England.

Blue is the color of relaxation and obviously also of healthy growth, a connection which should be considered for interior decorating in therapy rooms!

In the days when farming was more in accordance with natural laws, seeds were put onto a blue fabric and placed in the sun before being planted. This procedure charged the seed with the force of the sun and the blue energy later supported the healthy development of the plant.

Blue is best for relaxation, body and soul. It will make us breathe deeper and is a help against asthma. Blue relaxes the heart, reduces blood pressure and slows down our breathing. Blue supports weight gain, whilst red has the opposite effect. Blue aids short sightedness, whereas red aids long sightedness and effective eye strengthening charts have been developed as an aid, using this principle.

Overactive people should think of blue in their clothing and should visualise the breathing in of blue light. Blue is a very curative color, relaxes and reduces stress, provides the feeling of oneness and provides space for personal expression (orange). It also helps to ease claustrophobia and insecurity.

As the color of relaxation, blue should be used accordingly. Rooms full of stress should be painted in a blue shade, the same goes for rooms of relaxation and recovery, i.e. the bedroom. Blue provides the feeling of heavenly peace, safety and comfort. Light blue shades especially have this effect.

To make getting up easier after a relaxing night a friendly and activating painting should be placed on the wall opposite the bed or another opposite pole to blue should be created.

Indigo-blue is the color of the 3rd Eye-Chakra and too much of it can over stimulate it.

Dark-blue is associated with reliability and seriousness. The dark-blue suit, dark-blue limousines; basic color of many signs of "established" companies, as for example "Mercedes".

Blue is the favourite color of most adults.

In contrast to yellow, which has a shining character, blue has a deep character. Bright blues relate to the feeling of heaven and ease. Darker blue shades are associated with uncertainty and the unknown. This uncomfortable, uncertain depth is a very female principle. A depth and a silence in which the mysterious awaits us. Real undetected depth and real silence, to feel thrown back on oneself, to dive into oneself, to be alone with oneself is not everyone's favourite occupation, but in order to achieve greater knowledge and clarity for the searching, it must be recommended as the only option. In the end, in the depth, one finds connectedness with the whole.

Blue is the color of compassion and sympathy. Paintings of the great mother goddesses depicted their garments as blue, as for example Isis and the Mother Mary.

Violet

As a mixture of red and blue, it is a new quality between activity and relaxation. It is the color of higher love, respect and dignity towards oneself but also towards life. Violet is the color of internal knowledge and the understanding of life's myths and the power of white magic resulting from this.

Only if we can respect and accept ourselves can we understand ourselves, and only if we understand ourselves can we understand and live in harmony with the Cosmos. Violet is the color to support and symbolise these processes.

Being the color of the crown-chakra, the energy centre at the highest point of our head and our connection point to the cosmos, many spiritual people feel an urge towards violet from time to time. Violet has a high vibration and prepares the spiritually searching for bearing higher vibrations.

The negative aspect of violet is that it supports and can lead to snobbishness and arrogant behaviour. A sense of being "above others" can isolate. A good color to wear at funerals, for it lends dignity. As more thought generally should be given to the color utilised in hospital decor, apart from practical considerations, violet is an excellent color to be used in the entrance ways and halls. This supports the patient/visitor in feelings of sustaining dignity in a situation where too easily one feels out of control, or even a "number". The same goes for other institutions.

Violet-purple is the color for kings.

People with not enough feelings of self-worth should use violet from time to time. Also in suicidal periods it should be used to re-instate respect and love for life and oneself.

We all need violet from time to time and we should think of this when choosing clothing and furniture. We all have phases when we reject our emotions, our body, our doing and our thoughts and make ourselves look bad regarding ourselves as non-worthy human beings.

With violet we can learn to acknowledge ourselves as unique, wonderful individuals and worthy human beings under any circumstances.

Magenta

Magenta leads into a new dimension, to a new conscious-ness. Magenta is the color of release and rebirth, the "Phoe-nix from the Ashes". Attitudes which have been identified as being out of date can be released and eventually the release of our own physical body appears easier. It is always pre-sent if we have to distance ourselves from something in or around us.

Having this quality, magenta is an aid toward unblocking on all levels. It is recommended against depression, to trans-form dark energies and to recognise new dimensions of be-ing. But it is also a simple help for indigestion!

Magenta is especially required in new phases and meta-morphosis, particularly in periods of re-orientation and new beginnings. If violet, the new found knowledge ends and we long for red, the beginning of a new cycle, a point forms where from darkness magenta, the bridge, appears. If we acknowledge new wisdom, firstly a point of frustration with the existing old and accustomed is required (black) from which, supported by magenta, a new reality starts to form (red). Whereas yellow represents more mental and surface change, magenta represents deep cyclical and spir-itual change.

Magenta is the color of high consciousness (the purple of the bishop for example) and shows the ability to form life consciously.

Pink

Pink is the color of tenderness. Pink is, like the rose quartz stone, able to heal broken or hurt hearts and is as such of great importance. How much cruelty happens and how many hearts have been broken due to ignorance!

Children have not red, but pink in their Base-chakra. Due to this they cannot absorb pure red-dynamics, horror, anger, rage- and react accordingly with screams and shouts, in order to get rid of these hurting energies.

Only if the soul has been fully incarnated, normally after 21 years of age, is the personality in a position to learn to handle experiences of violence and aggression. Therefore violent films and the aggression of parents are energies which, for many youths, cannot be dealt with and which will leave a mark in their personality. Later, as an adult, they have to re-live this experience, hopefully better prepared and able to handle the confrontation, or reliving it in adult relationships.

It has been proven that abusive and brutal human beings relax considerably after a twenty minute stay in a "bubble-gum" colored room. However, one should not forget the necessity of the use of the complementary color, as people who stayed too long in these rooms ended up behaving even more violently than before.

Relating back to the rose quartz stone at the beginning of this section, it can be said that the healing qualities of stones can be pre-defined by their color.

Pink is the color of forgiveness or atonement. It is a mixture of red and white – desire and purity. One has to be wary of wanting to wear too much of it, thinking it is the color of service and love. Women in particular can end up negating their own needs and desires. Subconsciously, people often want to wear pink when they feel they need to be forgiven or to pull away from their angers or sexuality.

It is useful to surround an aggressive person with pink light (this to be done through mental projection) to help prevent not just damage to oneself, but to the aggressor also. Compassion – pink – comes from the heart level (or the Christ level) and therefore acts telepathically and with love.

White

Pure, reflecting all visible rays, but yet suggesting a feeling of sterility and isolation. Like black it is not really a color but an extreme. White is not a color of personality. People in white feel untouchable, one is without fault. This can help if one feels dirty. It can however also project the internal condition or one's wish to come across in that way.

A fashion crisis appeared some years ago. There was a lack of inspiration, and so extreme black and white colors were used as well as very fluorescent colors, the so-called neon colors.

White light is the light of Jesus Christ and it is recommended to surround oneself through visualisation with white light for protection before meditation.

Because of the clarity of its reflecting ability it is used for outer building walls in hot countries, and is also frequently used for traditional, ceremonial occasions.

Black

Black absorbs all rays. People with a strong need for attention and consideration will often wear black. Like all the other colors, black will manifest itself in the aura and can lead to catastrophic conditions as it will not provide any support to the living and changing processes of the personality if worn often.

Like white, black is not an expression of personality, which of course does not provide much opportunity for criticism. Black is very often preferred by highly creative people. It will create a vacuum in which the inspiration will find space by pushing the personality into the background.

Black is the darkness and emptiness, the mother from whom everything will grow. (Seeds germinate in the dark.)

If we look at black on a person, we cannot know what to expect. Due to this, the person wearing black is in control of the situation and the observer is challenged. This uncertainty can create an uncomfortable feeling. This is what many want to achieve, this certain position of power using black and the feeling of self-assurance. It is furthermore a sign of a person in fear and with the feeling of being endangered. In black we can find everything, it does not know limitations or borders, it is unpredictable. Something of deeper meaning can appear but also something relentlessly brutal. This uncertainty cannot only create fear, it is also interesting and mysterious. One does not know beforehand what it will look like, the "child" born from black.

Black also looks very formal, slimming and attractive and can achieve this result, especially in formal evening dress.

Grey

The color of denial, it is the most unremarkable color. The color of servility and of depression. On a grey background all other colors appear fresh and can create themselves best. Our environment should not be grey, it is too dull. If you have ever painted large surfaces grey, you will know about the dull effect of grey. Think how our pavements, roads and buildings are grey nowadays.....

Being the color of ash it is the color of complete destruction.

If a personality retreats from its environment, if he/she shuts down emotions, and if the internal power and joy for life and the lust and love for life are lost, this is internal suicide. The life functions and therefore the health will suffer, the mind becomes depressive, the body movements become slow and the person will speak in a monotone way:(if the person can lift themselves to do so) "I feel my life, my environment are only grey..." Such a person will hardly have the power and motivation to find a way out of this misery. It will depend on the persuasion of other people to make this person join a helping therapy. Orange will retrieve this person's sense of life and the joy of life, and will therefore open doors for further therapeutic steps.

Gold

Highest quality, highest knowledge. Gold reminds us of the highest perfection around us during periods of depression and despair. Gold is a very good healing color and we must not be mean with it.

It enriches every quality and every other color. Gold and silver are opposite poles like sun and moon, man and woman, day and night, hot and cold.

In Egypt, gold was used excessively and was considered the representative of highest wisdom and highest knowledge of the sun god Ra. It does not corrode, is therefore everlasting, incorruptible, thus the color of gods and kings(!?).

It seems interesting to investigate the expression "the golden shot" in relation to an overdose of heroin: All drugs change our mental condition. Technically this is shown in a slowing down of our brain vibration. They expose us to different realities, but not safely. Achieving access to these realities through meditation may be slower but definitely safer and in accordance with ones awareness level, character and life experience.

The average consciousness during the day (14-30Hz) is recognised in multicolor by the internal eye and is the brain vibration with which we stand in connection with the human empire. A relaxed condition has a brain frequency of 8-13 vibrations per second and will be seen as dark blue. The dream condition of the brain (4-7Hz) is normally only recognised by those mentally trained in consciousness- dream condition and as a sign, gold will become visible. As with a radio receiver this frequency changes in the human being according to the station we receive. We call it reality when the frequency changes. In a relaxed condition it is easily possible to communicate with the animal world and to see the world "through animal eyes". In the awake-dream condition we resonate ourselves into the world of plants. In the awake dreamless-deep sleep condition we are in resonance with the mineral world. The brain frequency is then 3-5Hz and the color is then nearly white with some magenta.

Experiments with drugs show that the whole field of human perception changes if the brain frequency changes only slightly. Further, these experiments showed that the state of mind alters the quality of the perceptions. It can be shocking, when awake, to experience new realities if unprepared and brought about through drugs.

It should become clearer why all religions stress mental and bodily cleanliness.

If I am frustrated, depressed or live in self pity, so will I draw equivalent experiences in my altered state, which will amplify my shock. "The golden shot" obviously has the effect of altering the consciousness to such an extent that the personality is confronted with unbearable realities. Due to that the body dies of shock. This happens on the golden level, because even for the properly mentally prepared, to experience when awake the state of the dreamless-sleep for the first time is safe only under guidance.

The way of meditation is the healthy way to become conscious. Searching the deep regions of the personality and leading them to a healthy wholeness in daily life is what we have to practice.

Drugs have been used in specific spiritual trainings – well prepared and under guidance – to explore new levels. Initiation also means becoming initiated into ones self. To be able to face oneself in all aspects. And this can be helped via "the golden way", the way of love and meditation.

Silver

It is reflective and has a connection with the moon and the changing flow of water and life. As the cycle of the moon is a cleansing and renewing one, so also is silver a cleansing color for the human, especially if used mentally. Silver transmits a feeling of reliability and stability. It is the color of the feminine principle, "the Queen" in mediaeval alchemy. It is, as with gold, associated with wisdom, but also with strong intuitive powers. Silver feels "lighter" than gold. Silver also creates an impression and feeling of speed – the 'Silver Arrow' is a famous fast racing car and Mercedes introduced silver as their branding color in their Formula 1 racing teams. Many cars also have silver looking wheel trims that speed along.... Gold has a more solid and stable feeling.

Brown

A very "earthy" and old color. As the color of autumn it shows hibernation and the dying process "back to earth". As humus it is the basis for new life; in a way one can say that brown asks for other colors. If there is no other color than brown in our life we live an undeveloped life. Brown is the color of convention, routine, safeness and concentration. It helps study but does not promote originality or imagination. It is a very conservative color. Somebody in a brown suit is somebody who is committed to his work, therefore reliable, even though he will find it not easy to make changes. As the color of wood it is a very good color for base materials. It helps develop patience and a healthy attitude to life, but it also supports the state of self denial and a feeling of low self worth.

Resources

Figures 1 – 4:

http://en.wikipedia.org/wiki/Theory_of_colors

Useful Books:

Theo Gimbel: "Healing Through Color" and "Form, Sound, Color and Healing" by The C.W.Daniel Company Ltd

Max Lüscher: "The Lüscher Color Test" (various tests by various publishers)

Rudolf Steiner: "Color" (more for 'insiders'), "Knowledge of the Higher Worlds",.... by Rudolf Steiner Press, London

Barbara Ann Brennan: "Hands of Light" by Bantam New Age Books. A very good book about Chakras and Healing; beautiful illustrations.

Books from White Eagle, e.g."Meditation", "Spiritual Unfoldment", "Wisdom from White Eagle", "Heal Thyself", "Book of Health and Healing",.... by the White Eagle Publishing Trust.

"MAP: The Co-Creative White Brotherhood Medical Assistance Program, Third Edition" by Machaelle Small Wright. Published by Perelandra, Ltd.

Useful Web Addresses:

International Color Association(ICA) http://www.aic-color.org

The International Association of Color (IAC) http://www.iac-color.co.uk

German Society of Color Science and Application
http://www.dfwg.de

AURASOMA (ASIACT) https://www.asiact.org

Dinshah Health Society http://www.dinshahhealth.org

Dr. Jacob Liberman: Cutting edge of light & color technology, blending physics and metaphysics
http://www.jacobliberman.org

The BIOPTRON Light Therapy: http://www.bioptron.eu

The College of Vibrational Medicine (UK)
http://www.collegeofvibrationalmedicine.org.uk

The White Eagle Lodge http://www.whiteagle.org

Institute of Complementary and Natural Medicine (UK)
http://icnm.org.uk

Crystal Herbs Ltd. Essences of high quality, e.g. Rainbow Light Body Essences

http://www.crystalherbs.com

National Federation of Spiritual Healers UK (Now known as The Healing Trust) http://www.thehealingtrust.org.uk

The Maitreya School of Healing
http://www.maitreyaschoolandhealingcentre.org.uk

Hygeia Eye Strengthening Chart
http://www.panosun.org/products.php?cat=35

PANGARDEN Game – To help you transform and answer life questions: www.pangarden.org

List of Personal Change Color Exercises

A Brighter Future!

The following exercise will help you brighten up your future. It utilises the power of color and visualisation to create a sense of optimism.

1. Imagine your future spreading out in front of you; Some people see a path extending out in front of them, others see a series of images leading off in front of them. If you could imagine seeing your future, what would that look like now?

2. Now, as you look at that representation of your future, imagine brightening up the vision by increasing the intensity of the colors in the image.

3. What happens if you allow your favourite optimistic color (gold?) to spread and shine throughout that future representation. Simply imagine spreading that color throughout your future. What is that like?

Rose Tinted Glasses

There is a common idiom in the English language; *"When someone is in love, they look at their partner through rose tinted glasses."* If you where to ask that person to describe their inner subjective experience you would discover that they actually color their internal image of their partner in a rose pink hue. This is one of the ways their mind codes their imagery so that they know, *"This is the person I love."*

We can use this knowledge to change our subjective experience of reality:

74

1. Think of something that you would like a new perspective on.

2. Select a resource that you would like to experience in the above. e.g.) Optimism, creativity, relaxation, happiness etc.

3. Represent that resource with a color.

4. Now imagine in front of you a pair of sunglasses which are colored with the color you selected in Step 3.

5. Put them on and look at the situation you selected in Step 1 with this new colored perspective.

6. Enjoy the new learnings you've gained. Perhaps try it again with other shades.

7. Would it be useful to have those shades on in future situations? Imagine a future situation, see what you would see and hear what you would hear as you imagine the situation through those colored shades...

Word Magic

The phrases that fly out of our mouths sometimes contain real magic that we can use to our benefit. Have you ever heard phrases such as:

- *"I saw it/him/her in a new light."*

- *"You have a bright future ahead of you."*

- *"The opportunity is golden!"*

- *"She had a kind of spiritual aura about her; electric blue/white"*

These phrases are Neuro-Linguistic processes, meaning the person's internal imagery is actually colored with what the words say. e.g.) *"The opportunity is golden!"* We can use this process to change our perceptions in a useful way:

Seeing People in a New Light

1. Think about an experience when you *"saw someone in a new light."*

2. Notice in your mind's eye what color that new light was.

3. Now think about someone currently in your life that you would benefit from seeing in a new light.

4. Imagine them in your mind and then see them in the new light. That is imagine them within the new light color.

5. Notice how this changes your perception of that person. And become aware of any new learnings.

Color Polarity Exercise

This exercise enables you to gain new perspectives on problems or stuck states of mind by representing the problem as a color and shape. You are then asked to represent the polar opposite of that with a new color and shape. Finally you combine these two polar opposites together which enables the mind to come up with new perspectives and insights into the problem.

1. Notice where in your body you feel the problem or stuck state.

2. If you were to give it a shape and color what would

that be like?

3. Set that aside for a moment and now think about what the opposite of that state is. e.g.) The opposite of *feeling stuck* could be *flying free*.

4. What shape and color is the opposite state?

5. Now imagine perceiving the shapes and colors of the two states together at the same time.

6. How quickly or slowly can you allow those to two states to merge together into a new shape and color?

7. Looking at that new shape and color, notice how your experience has changed.

8. Think about the original problem and notice new changes, perspectives or insights.

Color Wheel Exercise

You'll have seen the color wheel, on the next page, earlier in the book. Or you can go here to see a full screen version: http://www.effective-color.com

By allowing your eyes to gaze at a certain color, on the wheel, you will help to balance your overall Physical, Emotional, Mental and Spiritual (PEMS) levels.

A more advanced way of using the Color Wheel is to do the above exercise first and then hold an issue/problem you want to address in your mind while you allow your eyes to go to a color they feel drawn too. This way you give your system some overall balance first and then from that balance you get more input for a specific issue/problem.

Color Wheel (go here for a more detailed Color Wheel ==> http://www.effective-color.com**)**

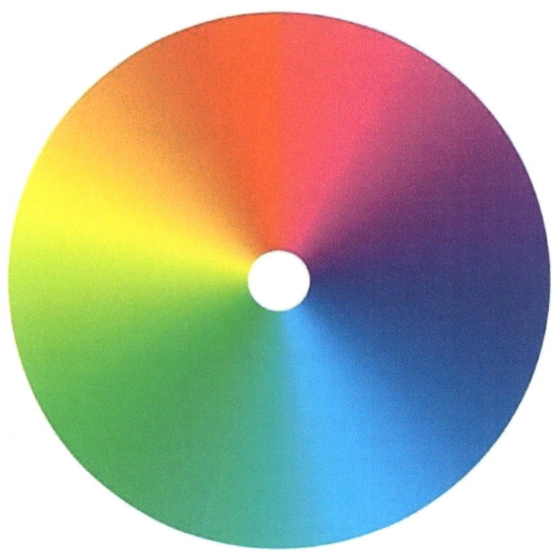

Color Energy Chakra Balancing Meditation

The following chakra meditation will help you balance your chakra energy system by imagining each chakra's color in turn starting with the color red at the root chakra and then working up through the other chakra's.

1. Find a comfortable position either sitting or laying down. Take a few deep clearing breaths and begin breathing slowly and evenly.

2. Visualise a golden light above your head and draw the light all the way down your body to your feet.

3. Imagine the light illuminating every part of your being.

4. As you allow yourself to become more and more re-

laxed, you can begin meditating on each chakra, starting with the Root Chakra. Meditate on the chakra's location, color and attributes as you work your way up each one to the Crown Chakra.

Root Chakra = Red; Base of the Spine

Splenic Chakra = Orange; Underneath the Navel

Solar Plexus Chakra = Yellow; Solar Plexus

The Heart Chakra = Green; Heart Centre

The Throat Chakra = Pale Blue; Throat

The Third Eye Chakra = Dark Blue; In-Between Eyes

The Crown Chakra = Violet; Top of Head

5. Closing the meditation properly is done by visualising the chakras one by one, starting at the top, closing like a flower. Finish your meditation by taking a few more deep breaths and imagine golden light filling your entire being from above.

www.ingramcontent.com/pod-product-compliance
Lightning Source LLC
Chambersburg PA
CBHW040831180526
45159CB00001B/148